POWER THROUGH
PRAYER

E.M. BOUNDS

Whitaker House

PITTSBURGH & COLFAX STREETS, SPRINGDALE, PA. 15144

POWER THROUGH PRAYER

ISBN: 0-88368-117-X
Printed in the United States of America
Copyright © 1982 by Whitaker House
Cover Photo © Josiah Davidson

Whitaker House
30 Hunt Valley Circle
New Kensington, PA 15068

10 11 12 13 14 15 16 17 / 06 05 04 03 02 01 00 99 98 97

CONTENTS

POWER THROUGH
PRAYER

Chapter 1

The Divine Channel
of Power

Study universal holiness of life. Your whole use-fulness depends on this, for your sermons last only an hour or two; your life preaches all week. If Satan can make you a covetous minister, a lover of praise, of pleasure, of good eating, he has ruined your ministry. Give yourself to prayer, and get your texts, your thoughts, your words from God. Luther spent his best three hours in prayer.

Robert Murray McCheyne

We are continually striving to create new methods, plans, and organizations to advance the Church. We are ever working to provide and stimulate growth and efficiency for the gospel.

This trend of the day has a tendency to lose sight of the man. Or else he is lost in the workings of the plan or organization. God's plan is to make much of the man, far more of him than of anything else. Men are God's method.

The Church is looking for better methods; God is looking for better men. "There was a man sent from God, whose name was John" (John 1:6). The dispensation which heralded and prepared the way for Christ was bound up in that man John. "Unto us a child is born, unto us a son is given" (Isaiah 9:6). The world's salvation comes out of that cradled Son.

When Paul appeals to the personal character of the men who rooted the gospel in the world, he solves the mystery of their success. The glory and efficiency of the gospel depend on the men who proclaim it. When God declares that "the eyes of the Lord run to and fro throughout the whole earth, to shew himself strong in the behalf of them whose heart is perfect toward him" (2 Chronicles 16:9), He declares the necessity of men. He acknowledges His dependence on them as a channel through which He can exert His power on the world.

This vital, urgent truth is one that this age of machinery is apt to forget. The forgetting of it is as detrimental to the Word of God as removing the sun from its sphere would be. Darkness, confusion, and death would ensue.

What the Church needs today is not more or better machinery, not new organizations or more and novel methods. She needs men whom the Holy Spirit can use—men of prayer, men mighty *in* prayer. The Holy Spirit does not flow through methods, but through men. He does not come on machinery, but on men. He does not anoint plans, but men—men of prayer!

An eminent historian has said that the accidents of personal character have more to do with the revolutions of nations than either philosophic historians or democratic politicians will allow. This truth fully applies to the gospel of Christ, and the character and conduct of the followers of Christ— Christianize the world, and you transfigure nations and individuals. It is eminently true of the preachers of the gospel.

The character as well as the fortunes of the gospel are committed to the preacher. He either makes or mars the message from God to man. The preacher is the golden pipe through which the divine oil flows. The pipe must not only be golden, but open and flawless. This way the oil may have a full, unhindered, and unwasted flow.

The man makes the preacher. God must make the man. The messenger is, if possible, more than the message. The preacher is more than the sermon. The preacher *makes* the sermon. As life-giving milk from the mother's bosom is no more than the mother's life, so all the preacher *says* is tinctured, impregnated, by what the preacher *is*. The treasure is in earthen vessels, and the taste of the vessel may permeate and discolor the treasure. The man—the whole man—lies behind the sermon. Preaching is not the performance of an hour. It is the outflow of a life. It takes twenty years to make a sermon, because it takes twenty years to make the man. The true sermon is a thing of life. The sermon grows because the man grows. The sermon is forceful because the man is forceful. The sermon is holy because the man is holy. The sermon is full of the divine anointing because the man is full of the divine anointing.

Paul termed it "my gospel." It was not that he had slanted it with his personal eccentricities or selfish understanding. But, the gospel was laid up in the heart and lifeblood of Paul as a personal trust to be executed by his Pauline traits—to be set aflame and empowered by the fiery energy of his fiery soul. Paul's sermons—what were they? Where are they? Skeletons, scattered fragments, afloat on the sea of inspiration! But the man Paul—greater than his sermons—lives forever, in full form, feature, and stature, with his molding hand on the Church. The preacher is only a voice. The voice in silence dies; the text is forgotten; the sermon fades from memory; but the preacher lives.

In its life-giving forces, the sermon cannot rise above the man. Dead men preach dead sermons, and dead sermons kill. Everything depends on the spiritual character of the preacher. Under the Jewish dispensation, the high priest had "Holiness to the Lord" inscribed in jeweled letters on a golden frontlet. So every preacher in Christ's ministry must be molded into and mastered by this same holy motto. It is a shame that the Christian ministry has less holiness of character and aim than the Jewish priesthood. Jonathan Edwards, the famous missionary, said, "I went on with my eager pursuit after more holiness and conformity to Christ. The heaven I desired was a heaven of holiness."

The gospel of Christ does not move by popular waves. It has no self-propagating power. It moves as the men who have charge of it move. The preacher must live the gospel. Its divine, most distinctive features must be embodied in him. The constraining power of love must be in the preacher as a projecting, extraordinary, all-commanding, and self-oblivious force. The energy of self-denial must be his being—his heart, blood, and bones. He must go forth as a man among men, clothed with humility, abiding in meekness, wise as a serpent, and harmless as a dove. He must wear the bonds of a servant with the spirit of a king, and the simplicity and sweetness of a child.

The preacher must throw himself—with all the abandon of a perfect, self-emptying faith and a self-consuming zeal—into his work for the salvation of men. The men who take hold of and shape a generation for God must be hearty, heroic, compassionate, and fearless martyrs. If they are timid timeservers, place-seekers, men-pleasers, men-fearers, if their faith in God or His Word is weak, and if their denial may be broken by any phrase of self or the world, they cannot take hold of the Church or the world for God.

The preacher's sharpest and strongest preaching should be to himself. His most difficult, delicate, laborious, and thorough work must be with himself. The training of the twelve was the great, difficult, and enduring work of Christ. Preachers are not sermon-makers, but men-makers, and saint-makers. Only he who has made himself a man and a saint is well-trained for this business. God does not need great talents, great learning, or great preachers, but men great in holiness, great in faith, great in love, great in fidelity, great for God. He needs men who are always preaching holy sermons in the pulpit, and living holy lives out of it. These can mold a great generation for God.

After this order, the early Christians were formed. They were men of solid mold, preachers after the heavenly type—heroic, stalwart, soldierly, saintly. To them, preaching meant self-denying, self-crucifying, serious, toilsome, martyr business. They applied themselves to it in a way that influenced their generation, and formed in its womb a genera-tion yet unborn for God. The preaching man is to be the praying man. Prayer is the preacher's mightiest weapon. An almighty force in itself, it gives life and force to all.

The real sermon is made in the closet. The man— God's man—is made in the closet. His life and his most profound convictions are born in his secret communion with God. The burdened and tearful agony of his spirit, his weightiest and sweetest messages are received when alone with God. Prayer makes the man; prayer makes the preacher; prayer makes the pastor.

The pulpit of this day is weak in praying. The pride of learning is in opposition to the dependent humility of prayer. In the pulpit, prayer is all too often only official—a performance for the routine of service. In the modern pulpit, prayer is not the mighty force it was in Paul's life or ministry. Every preacher who does not make prayer a mighty factor in his own life and ministry is weak as a factor in God's work, and is powerless to advance God's cause in this world.

Chapter 2

Our Sufficiency Is of God

But above all he excelled in prayer. The inwardness and weight of his spirit, the reverence and solemnity of his address and behavior, and the fewness and fullness of his words have often struck even strangers with admiration as they used to reach others with consolation. The most awful living, reverend frame I ever felt or beheld, I must say was his prayer. And truly it was a testimony. He knew and lived nearer to the Lord than other men, for they that know Him most will see most reason to approach Him with reverence and fear.

William Penn of George Fox

By a slight perversion, the sweetest graces may bear the bitterest fruit. The sun gives life, but sun-strokes are death. Preaching is to give life, but it may kill. The preacher holds the keys; he may lock as well as unlock. Preaching is God's great institution for the planting and maturing of spiritual life. When properly executed, its benefits are untold. When wrongly executed, no evil can exceed its damaging results.

It is an easy matter to destroy the flock if the shepherd is unwary or the pasture is destroyed. It is easy to capture the citadel if the watchmen are asleep or the food and water are poisoned. Invested with such gracious prerogatives, exposed to great evils, involving so many grave responsibilities, it would be a parody on the shrewdness of the devil—a libel on his character and reputation—if he did not use his master influences to adulterate the preacher and the preaching. In the face of all this, Paul's exclamatory question, "Who is sufficient for these things?" (2 Corinthians 2:16) is never out of place.

Paul says, "Our sufficiency is of God; who also hath made us able ministers of the new testament; not of the letter, but of the spirit: for the letter killeth, but the spirit giveth life" (2 Corinthians 3:5-6). The true ministry is God-touched, God-enabled, and God-made. The Spirit of God is on the preacher in anointing power. The fruit of the Spirit is in his heart. The Spirit of God has vitalized the man and the word; his preaching gives life, gives life as the spring gives life. His words give life as the resurrection gives life. His sermons give ardent life as the summer gives ardent life. His preaching gives fruitful life as the autumn gives fruitful life. The life-giving preacher is a man of God, whose soul is continually following after God. His eye looks only to God, and in him, by the power of God's Spirit, the flesh and the world have been crucified. His ministry is like the generous flood of a life-giving river.

The preaching which kills is nonspiritual preaching. The ability of the preaching is not from God. Lower sources than God have given it energy and stimulant. The Spirit is not evident in the preacher nor his preaching. Many kinds of forces may be projected and stimulated by preaching which kills, but they are not spiritual forces. They may resemble spiritual forces, but are only the shadow, the counterfeit. They may seem to have life, but the life is false. The preaching which kills is the letter. It may be shapely and orderly, but it is the letter still—the dry, husky letter, the empty, bald shell. The letter may have the germ of life in it, but it has no breath of spring to evoke it. They are winter seeds, as hard as the winter's soil, as icy as the winter's air. They will neither thaw nor germinate.

This letter-preaching has the truth. But even divine truth has no life-giving energy alone. It must be energized by the Spirit, with all God's forces behind it. Truth unquickened by God's Spirit deadens as much as, or more than, error. It may be the truth, but without the Spirit its shade and touch are deadly. Its truth is error, its light darkness. The letter-preaching is unanointed, neither mellowed nor oiled by the Spirit.

There may be tears, but tears cannot run God's machinery. Tears may be nothing but superficial expression. There may be feelings and earnestness, but it is the emotion of the actor and the earnestness of the attorney. The preacher may be moved by the kindling of his own sparks, be eloquent over his own exegesis, and earnest in delivering the product of his own brain, but the message of his words may be dead and fruitless. The professor may imitate the fire of the apostles; brains and nerves may feign the work of God's Spirit, and by these forces the letter may glow and sparkle like an illuminated text, but the glow and sparkle will be as barren as the field sown with pearls. The death-dealing element lies behind the words, behind the sermon, behind the occasion, behind the manner, behind the action.

The great hindrance is in the preacher himself. He does not find within himself the mighty, life-creating forces. There may be no deficiency in his orthodoxy, honesty, cleanness, or earnestness. But, somehow the man—the inner man—in his secret places has never broken down and surrendered to God. His inner life is not a great highway for the transmission of God's message, God's power.

Somehow, self, not God, rules in the holy of holies. Somewhere, all unconscious to himself, some spiritual nonconductor has touched his inner being. The divine current has been arrested. His inner being has never felt its thorough spiritual bankruptcy, its utter powerlessness. He has never learned to cry out with an ineffable cry of self-despair and helplessness until God's power and fire come in, fill, purify, and empower. Self-esteem—self-ability in some wicked form—has defamed and violated the temple which should be held sacred for God.

Life-giving preaching costs the preacher much—death to self, crucifixion to the world, the travail of his own soul. Only crucified preaching can give life. Crucified preaching can only come from a crucified man.

Chapter 3

Man's Most Noble Exercise

During this affliction I examined my life in relation to eternity closer than I had done when in the enjoyment of health. In the examination relative to the discharge of my duties toward my fellow-men as a man, a Christian minister, and an officer of the Church, I stood approved by my own conscience. But, in relation to my Redeemer and Savior, the result was different. My returns of gratitude and loving obedience bear no proportion to my obligations for redeeming, persevering, and supporting me through the vicissitudes of life from infancy to old age. The coldness of my love to Him who first loved me and has done so much for me overwhelmed and confused me. And, to complete my unworthy character, I had not only neglected to improve the grace given to the extent of my duty and privilege, but for want of that improvement had, while abounding in perplexing care and labor, declined from first zeal and love. I was confounded, humbled myself, implored mercy, and renewed my covenant to strive and devote myself unreservedly to the Lord.

Bishop McKendree

The preaching which kills may be, and often is, orthodox—dogmatically, inviolably orthodox. We love orthodoxy. It is good. It is the best. It is the clean, clear-cut teaching of God's Word. It is the trophies won by truth in its conflict with error, the levees which faith has raised against the desolating floods of honest or reckless misbelief or unbelief. But, orthodoxy, clear and hard as a crystal, suspicious and militant, may be nothing but the letter, well-shaped, well-named, and well-learned—the letter which kills. Nothing is so dead as a dead orthodoxy—too dead to speculate, too dead to think, study, or pray.

The preaching which kills may have insight and grasp of principle. It may be scholarly and critical in taste. It may be fluent in all the minor details of the derivation and grammar of the letter. It may be able to trim the letter into its perfect pattern, and illuminate it as Plato and Cicero may have done. It may study the letter as a lawyer studies his textbooks to form his brief or to defend his case. And yet, it may still be like a frost, a killing frost. Letter-preaching may be eloquent, embellished with poetry and rhetoric, sprinkled with prayer, spiced with sensation, illuminated by genius, and yet these may merely be the chaste, costly mountings—the rare and beautiful flowers—which coffin the corpse.

The preaching which kills may be without scholarship. It may be unmarked by any freshness of thought or feeling, clothed in tasteless generalities or dull specialities. It may be slovenly, savoring neither of closet nor of study, graced neither by thought, nor expression, nor prayer. Under such preaching, how wide and utter the desolation! How profound the spiritual death!

This letter-preaching deals with the surface and shadow of things, not the things themselves. It does not penetrate the inner part. It has no deep insight into, no strong grasp of, the hidden life of God's Word. It is true to the outside. But, the outside is the hull which must be broken and penetrated to obtain the kernel. The letter may be dressed so as to attract and be fashionable, but the attraction is not toward God, nor is the fashion for heaven.

The failure is in the preacher. God has not made him. He has never been in the hands of God like clay in the hands of the potter. He has been busy working on the sermon, its thought and finish, its drawing and impressive forces. But, the deep things of God have never been sought, studied, fathomed, experienced by him. He has never stood before "the throne, high and lifted up" (Isaiah 6:1). He has never heard the seraphim song, seen the vision, nor felt the rush of that awesome holiness. He has never cried out in utter abandon and despair under the sense of weakness and guilt. He has never had his life renewed, his heart touched, purged, and inflamed by the live coal from God's altar.

His ministry may draw people to him, to the Church, and to the form and ceremony. But, no true drawings to God, no sweet, holy, divine communion are induced. The Church has been adorned, but not edified. It has pleased, but not sanctified. Life is suppressed. The city of our God becomes the city of the dead—the Church a graveyard, not an embattled army. Praise and prayer are stifled; worship is dead. The preacher and the preaching have helped sin, not holiness. They have populated hell, not heaven.

Preaching which kills is prayerless preaching. Without prayer, the preacher creates death and not life. The preacher who is feeble in prayer is feeble in life-giving forces. The preacher who has retired from prayer as a conspicuous and largely prevailing element in his own character has stripped his preaching of its distinctive, life-giving power. There is and will be professional praying, but professional praying helps the preaching to do its deadly work. Professional praying chills and kills both preaching and praying.

Much of the lax devotion and lazy, irreverent attitudes in congregational praying is attributable to professional praying in the pulpit. The prayers in many pulpits are long, discursive, dry, and inane. Without anointing or heart, they fall like a killing frost on all the graces of worship. Death-dealing prayers they are. Every trace of devotion has perished under their breath. The more dead they are the longer they grow.

A plea for short praying, live praying, real heart praying, praying by the Holy Spirit—direct, specific, ardent, simple, anointed in the pulpit—is in order. A school to teach preachers how to pray, as God counts praying, would be more beneficial to true piety, true worship, and true preaching than all theological schools.

Stop! Pause! Consider! Where are we? What are we doing? Preaching to kill? Praying to kill? Praying to God! The great God, the Maker of all worlds, the Judge of all men! What reverence! What simplicity! What sincerity! What truth in the inward parts is demanded! How real we must be! How hearty! Prayer to God: the most noble exercise, the loftiest effort of man, the most real thing! We will forever discard accursed preaching and prayer which kill and do the real thing. Life-creating preaching brings the mightiest force to bear on heaven and earth. It draws on God's exhaustless and open treasure for the need and beggary of man.

Chapter 4

Talking to God For Men

Let us often look at Brainerd, an American missionary to the native Indians, in the woods of America pouring out his very soul before God for the perishing heathen without whose salvation nothing could make him happy. Prayer—secret, fervent, believing prayer—lies at the root of all personal godliness. A competent knowledge of the language where a missionary lives, a mild and winning temper, a heart given up to God in close religion—these, these are the attainments which, more than all knowledge or all other gifts, will fit us to become the instruments of God in the great work of human redemption.

Carey's Brotherhood
Serampore, India

There are two extreme tendencies in the ministry. The one is to shut itself out from fellowship with the people. The monk and the hermit are illustrations of this. They shut themselves out from men to be more with God. They failed, of course. Our being with God is of use only as we expend its priceless benefits on men.

Too often Christian leaders shut themselves in their studies and become students—bookworms, Bible experts, and sermon makers. They are noted for literature, thought, and sermons; but the people and God, where are they? Out of heart, out of mind. Preachers who are great thinkers, great students, must be the greatest of pray-ers. If they are not, they will be the greatest of backsliders, heartless professionals, rationalistic, less than the least of preachers in God's estimate.

The other tendency is to popularize the ministry thoroughly. It is no longer God's, but a ministry of affairs, of the people. The minister does not pray because his mission is to the people. If he can move the people, create a sensation in favor of religion, and an interest in church work—he is satisfied. His personal relationship to God is no factor in his work. Prayer has little or no place in his plans. The disaster and ruin of such a ministry cannot be computed by earthly mathematics. What the preacher is in prayer to God—for himself, for his people—so is his power for real good to men, his true fruitfulness, and his true fidelity to God—for time and for eternity.

It is impossible for the preacher to keep his spirit in harmony with the divine nature of his high calling without much and constant prayer. It is a serious mistake to think that the preacher, by duty and laborious fidelity to the work and routine of the ministry, can keep himself trim and fit for his high calling. Even sermon-making—incessant and taxing as an art, as a duty, as a work, or as a pleasure—will engross, harden, and estrange the heart from God by neglect of prayer. The scientist loses God in nature. The preacher may lose God in his sermon.

Prayer freshens the heart of the preacher, keeps it in tune with God, and in sympathy with the people. It lifts his ministry out of the chilly air of a profession, revitalizes routine, and moves every wheel with the ease and power of a divine anointing.

Mr. Spurgeon says: "Of course the preacher is above all others distinguished as a man of prayer. He prays as an ordinary Christian, else he were a hypocrite. He prays more than ordinary Christians, else he were disqualified for the office he has undertaken. If you as ministers are not very prayerful, you are to be pitied. If you become lax in sacred devotion, not only will you need to be pitied but your people also, and the day approaches in which you will be ashamed and confounded. All our libraries and studies are mere emptiness compared with our closets. Our seasons of fasting and prayer at the Tabernacle have been high days indeed; never has heaven's gate stood wider; never have our hearts been nearer the central glory."

The praying which makes a prayerful ministry is not the meager praying added only as flavoring to give it a pleasant taste. But, the praying must be in the body, form, blood, and bones. Prayer is no petty duty put into a corner. It is no piecemeal performance made out of the fragments of time which have been snatched from business and other engagements of life. The best of our time, and the heart of our time and strength must be given to prayer. It does not mean that the closet is absorbed in the study or swallowed up in the activities of ministerial duties. But, it means the closet first, the study and activities second. In this way, both the study and the activities are freshened and made efficient by the closet. Prayer that affects one's ministry must touch one's life. The praying which gives color and bent to character is no pleasant, hurried pastime. It must enter as strongly into the heart and life as Christ's "strong crying and tears" did (Hebrews 5:7). It must draw the soul into an agony of desire as Paul's did. It must be an inwrought fire and force like the "effectual fervent prayer" of James (James 5:16). The praying must be of that quality which, when put into the golden censer and incensed before God, works mighty, spiritual struggles and revolutions.

Prayer is not a little habit pinned onto us while we were tied to our mother's apron strings. Neither is it a little, decent quarter of a minute's grace said over an hour's dinner. But, it is a most serious work of our most serious years. It engages more of time and appetite than our longest dinings or richest feasts. The prayer that makes much of our preaching must itself be made much of. The character of our praying will determine the character of our preaching. Light praying will make light preaching. Prayer makes preaching strong, gives it an anointing, and makes it stick. In every ministry righteously working for good, prayer has always been a serious business.

The preacher must primarily be a man of prayer. In the school of prayer, only the heart can learn to preach. No learning can make up for the failure to pray. No earnestness, no diligence, no study, no gifts will supply its lack.

Talking to men for God is a great thing, but talking to God for men is still greater. He who has not learned well how to talk to God for men will never talk well—with real success—to men for God. More than this, prayerless words, both in and out of the pulpit are deadening.

Chapter 5

How to Get Results For God

You know the value of prayer: it is precious beyond all price. Never, never neglect it.

Sir Thomas Buxton

Prayer is the first thing, the second thing, the third thing necessary to a minister. Pray, then, my dear brother; pray, pray, pray.

Edward Payson

Prayer, in the preacher's life, study, and pulpit, must be a conspicuous and all-impregnating force, and an all-coloring ingredient. It must play no secondary role, be no mere coating. The preacher is called to be with his Lord "all night in prayer." To train himself in self-denying prayer, he is charged to look to his Master, who, "rising up a great while before day,... went out, and departed into a solitary place, and there prayed" (Mark 1:35).

The preacher's study ought to be a closet, a Bethel, an altar, a vision, and a ladder, so that every thought might ascend heavenward before it goes manward. Likewise, every part of the sermon should be scented by the air of heaven and made serious, because God was in the study.

Just as the steam engine never moves until the fire is kindled, so preaching—with all its machinery, perfection, and polish—is at a dead standstill, spiritually, until prayer has kindled and created the steam. The texture, fineness, and strength of the sermon are rubbish unless the mighty impulse of prayer is in it, through it, and behind it. The preacher must, by prayer, put God in the sermon. The preacher must, by prayer, move God toward the people before he can move the people to God by his words. The preacher must have had audience and ready access to God before he can have access to the people. An open way to God for the preacher is the surest pledge of an open way to the people.

It is necessary to iterate and reiterate that prayer,

as a mere habit, as a performance gone through by routine or in a professional way, is a dead and rotten thing. Such praying has no connection with the praying for which we plead. We stress true praying which engages and sets on fire every high element of the preacher's being. We emphasize prayer which is born of vital oneness with Christ in the fullness of the Holy Spirit, and which springs from the deep, overflowing fountains of His tender compassion.

We seek prayer composed of undying solicitude for man's eternal good, and a consuming zeal for the glory of God. The preacher needs a thorough conviction of his difficult and delicate work and of his imperative need of God's mightiest help. Praying grounded on these solemn and profound convictions is the only true praying. Preaching backed by such praying is the only preaching which sows the seeds of eternal life in human hearts, and builds men up for heaven.

It is true that—with little or no praying—there may be popular, pleasant, captivating, and intellectual preaching which avails a small amount of good. But, the preaching which secures God's end in preaching must be born of prayer from the initial conception to the actual presentation. It must be delivered with the energy and spirit of prayer. It must be followed, made to germinate, and kept in vital force in the hearts of the hearers by the preacher's prayers, long after the occasion has passed.

We may excuse the spiritual poverty of our preaching in many ways. But, the true reason for it is the lack of urgent prayer for God's presence in the power of the Holy Spirit. There are innumerable preachers who can deliver masterful sermons, but the effects are shortlived. They do not affect the regions of the spirit where the fearful war between God and Satan, heaven and hell, is being waged, because they are not made powerfully militant and spiritually victorious by prayer.

The preachers who gain mighty results for God are the men who have prevailed in their pleadings with God *before* venturing to plead with men. The preachers who are the mightiest in their closets with God are the mightiest in their pulpits with men.

Preachers are human folks, and are often exposed to—involved in—the strong currents of human emotions and problems. Praying is spiritual work, and human nature does not like taxing, spiritual work. Human nature wants to sail to heaven under a pleasant breeze, and a full, smooth sea. Prayer is humbling work. It abases intellect and pride, crucifies vainglory, and signals our spiritual bankruptcy. All these are hard for flesh and blood to bear. It is easier not to pray than to bear them. So, we come to one of the crying evils of these times, maybe of all times—little or no praying. Of these two evils, perhaps little praying is worse than no praying. Little praying is a kind of make-believe, a salve for the conscience, a farce and a delusion.

The little regard we give prayer is evident from the little time we spend in it. The time given to prayer by the average preacher scarcely counts in light of how the remaining time is delegated to daily chores. Not infrequently, the preacher's only praying is by his bedside—in his nightdress, ready for bed. Perchance, he gets in a few additional prayers before he is dressed in the morning. How feeble, vain, and little is such praying compared with the time and energy devoted to praying by holy men in and out of the Bible! How poor and meager our petty, childish praying is beside the habits of the true men of God in all ages! God commits the keys of His Kingdom to men who think that praying is their main business, and devote time to it according to this high estimate of its importance. By these men, He works His spiritual wonders in this world. Great praying is the sign and seal of God's great leaders. It is the most earnest of the conquering forces with which God will crown their labors.

The preacher is commissioned to pray as well as to preach. His mission is incomplete if he does not do both well. The preacher may speak with all the eloquence of men and of angels, but unless he can pray with a faith which draws all heaven to his aid, his preaching will be "as sounding brass or a tinkling cymbal." It will be useless for permanent, God-honoring, soul-saving purposes.

Chapter 6

Great Men of Prayer

The principal cause of my leanness and unfruitfulness is due to an unaccountable backwardness to pray. I can write or read or converse or hear with a ready heart. But, prayer is more spiritual and inward than any of these, and the more spiritual any duty is, the more my carnal heart is apt to stray from it. Prayer and patience and faith are never disappointed. I have long since learned that if ever I was to be a minister, faith and prayer must make me one. When I can find my heart dissolved in prayer, everything else is comparatively easy.

Richard Newton

It may be considered a spiritual axiom that, in every truly successful ministry, prayer is an evident and controlling force. It is evident and controlling in the life of the preacher, evident and controlling in the deep spirituality of his work. A ministry may be a very thought provoking ministry without prayer. The preacher may secure fame and popularity without prayer. The whole machinery of the preacher's life and work may be run without the oil of prayer, or with scarcely enough to grease one cog. But, no ministry can be a spiritual one—securing holiness in the preacher and in his people— without prayer being made an evident and controlling force.

Indeed, the preacher who prays puts God into the work. God does not come into the preacher's work as a matter of course or on general principle. But, He comes in by prayer and special urgency. It is as true of the preacher as of the penitent that God will be found the day that we seek Him with the whole heart. A prayerful ministry is the only ministry that brings the preacher into sympathy with the people. As essentially as prayer unites the human, it does the divine. A prayerful ministry is the only ministry qualified for the high offices and responsibilities of the preacher. Colleges, knowledge, books, theology, and preaching do not make a preacher, but praying does. The apostles' commission to preach was nothing until it was filled up by the praying which Pentecost resulted from. A prayerful minister has passed beyond the regions of the popular—beyond the man of mere affairs, secularities, and pulpit attractiveness. He has passed beyond the ecclesiastical organizer or leader, and has entered into a more sublime and mightier region—the region of the spiritual.

Holiness is the product of the prayerful preacher's work. Transfigured hearts and lives emblazon the reality of his work, its trueness and substantial nature. God is with him. His ministry is not based or built on worldly, surface principles. He is highly experienced and deeply learned in the things of God. His long, deep communings with God about His people and the agony of his wrestling spirit have crowned him as a prince in the things of God. The iciness of mere professionalism has long since melted under the intensity of his praying.

The superficial results of many a ministry, and the deadness of others are to be found in the lack of praying. No ministry can succeed without much praying, and this praying must be fundamental, ever-abiding, ever-increasing. The text—the sermon—should be the result of prayer. The study should be bathed in prayer, all its duties impregnated with prayer, its whole spirit the spirit of prayer.

"I am sorry that I have prayed so little" was the deathbed regret of one of God's chosen ones. That is a sad and remorseful regret for a preacher. "I want a life of greater, deeper, truer prayer," said the late Archbishop Tait. So may we all say, and this may we all secure.

God's true preachers can be distinguished by one great feature: they are men of prayer. Often differing in many things, they have always had a common center. They may have started from different points, and traveled by different roads, but they converge to one point: they are one in prayer. To them, God is the center of attraction, and prayer is the path which led to God. These men do not pray occasionally— not a little or at odd times. But, they so pray that their prayers enter into and shape their very characters. They pray so as to affect their own lives, the lives of others, and to make the history of the Church influence the current of the times. They spend much time in prayer, not because they watch the shadow on the dial or the hands on the clock, but because it is to them so momentous and engaging a business that they can scarcely quit.

Prayer is to them what it was to Paul—a striving with earnest effort of soul. It is to them what it was to Jacob—a wrestling and prevailing. It is to them what it was to Christ—strong crying and tears. They pray "always with all prayer and supplication in the Spirit, and watching thereunto with all perseverance" (Ephesians 6:18). "The effectual fervent prayer" has been, and still is, the mightiest weapon of God's mightiest soldiers.

The statement in regard to Elijah—that he "was a man subject to like passions as we are, and he prayed earnestly that it might not rain: and it rained not on the earth by the space of three years and six months. And he prayed again, and the heaven gave rain, and the earth brought forth her fruit" (James 5:17-18)—applies to all prophets and preachers who have moved their generation for God, and shows the instrument by which they worked their wonders.

Many private prayers must be short. Public prayers, as a rule, ought to be short and condensed. And, there is often need for spontaneous, exclamatory prayer. However, in our private communions with God, time is essential to the value of the prayer. Much time spent with God is the secret of all successful praying.

Prayer which produces a powerful influence is the mediate or immediate product of much time spent with God. Our short prayers are effective and efficient because long ones have preceded them. The short, prevailing prayer cannot be prayed by one who has not prevailed with God in a mightier struggle of long continuance. Jacob's victory of faith could not have been gained without that all-night wrestling. God's acquaintance is not made hurriedly. He does not bestow His gifts on the casual or hasty comer and goer. To be much alone with God is the secret of knowing Him and of having influence with Him. He yields to the persistency of a faith that knows Him. He bestows His richest gifts on those who declare their desire for and appreciation of those gifts by the constancy as well as earnestness of their importunity.

Christ, who in this as well as in other things is our Example, spent many whole nights in prayer. His custom was to pray much. He had His habitual place to pray. Many long seasons of praying make up His history and character. Paul prayed day and night. Daniel's three daily prayers took time away from other important interests. David's morning, noon, and night praying was doubtless on many occasions very long and involved. While we have no specific account of the time these Bible saints spent in prayer, the indications are that they devoted much time to prayer, and on some occasions long seasons of praying were their custom.

We would not want anyone to think that the value of their prayers is measured by the clock. Our purpose is to impress on our minds the necessity of being much alone with God. And, if this feature has not been produced by our faith, then our faith is feeble and superficial.

The men who have most fully imitated Christ in their character, and have most powerfully affected the world for Him, have been men who spent so much time with God as to make it a notable feature of their lives. Charles Simeon, the English revivalist, devoted the hours from four to eight in the morning to God. John Wesley spent two hours a day in prayer. He began at four in the morning. One who knew him well wrote: "He thought prayer to be more his business than anything else, and I have seen him come out of his closet with a serenity of face next to shining."

John Fletcher, an English clergyman and author, stained the walls of his room by the breath of his prayers. Sometimes he would pray all night—always, frequently, and with great earnestness. His whole life was a life of prayer. "I would not rise from my seat," he said, "without lifting my heart to God." His greeting to a friend was always: "Do I meet you praying?" Martin Luther said: "If I fail to spend two hours in prayer each morning, the devil gets the victory through the day. I have so much business I cannot get on without spending three hours daily in prayer." He had a motto: "He that has prayed well has studied well."

Archbishop Leighton was so much alone with God that he seemed to be in a perpetual meditation. "Prayer and praise were his business and his pleasure," says his biographer. Bishop Ken was so much with God that his soul was said to be God-enamored. He was with God before the clock struck three every morning. Bishop Asbury said: "I propose to rise at four o'clock as often as I can and spend two hours in prayer and meditation." Samuel Rutherford, the fragrance of whose piety is still rich, rose at three in the morning to meet God in prayer. Joseph Alleine, an English clergyman, arose at four o'clock for his business of praying until eight. If he heard other tradesmen going about their business before he was up, he would exclaim: "Oh, how this shames me! Does *my* Master not deserve more than theirs?" He who has well learned this practice of prayer draws to it at will, on sight, and with the acceptance of heaven's unfailing bank.

One of the holiest and most gifted of Scottish preachers said: "I ought to spend the best hours in communion with God. It is my noblest and most fruitful employment, and is not to be thrust into a corner. The morning hours, from six to eight, are the most uninterrupted and should be thus employed. After tea is my best hour, and that should be solemnly dedicated to God. I ought not to give up the good and old habit of prayer before going to bed; but guard must be kept against sleep. When I awake in the night, I ought to rise and pray. A little time after breakfast might be given to intercession." This was the praying plan of Robert Murray McCheyne. In their praying, the memorable Methodists shame us. "From four to five in the morning, private prayer; from five to six in the evening, private prayer."

John Welch, the holy and wonderful Scottish preacher, thought the day was ill-spent if he did not spend eight or ten hours in prayer. He kept a blanket near his bed so that he might wrap himself when he arose to pray at night. His wife would complain when she found him lying on the ground weeping. He would reply: "O woman, I have the souls of three thousand to answer for, and I do not know how it is with many of them!"

Bishop Wilson said: "In H. Martyn's journal, the spirit of prayer—the time he devoted to the duty—

and his fervor in it are the first things which strike me."

Payson wore grooves into the hard-wood floor where his knees pressed so often and so long. His biographer says: "His continuing time in prayer, regardless of his circumstances, is the most noticeable fact in his history. It points out the duty of all who would rival his eminency. To his ardent and persevering prayers must no doubt be ascribed in a great measure his distinguished and almost uninterrupted success."

The Marquis DeRenty, to whom Christ was most precious, ordered his servant to call him from his devotions at the end of half an hour. The servant at the time saw his face through an opening. It was marked with such holiness that he hated to arouse him. His lips were moving, but he was perfectly silent. The servant waited until an hour and a half had passed, then he called to him. The Marquis arose from his knees, saying that half an hour was so short when he was communing with Christ.

Brainerd said: "I love to be alone in my cottage, where I can spend much time in prayer."

William Bramwell is famous in Methodist records for personal holiness, for his wonderful success in preaching, and for the marvelous answers to his prayers. He would pray for hours at a time. He almost lived on his knees. He went over his circuits like a flame of fire. The fire was kindled by the time he spent in prayer. He often spent as much as four hours in a single season of prayer in retirement.

Bishop Andrewes spent the greatest part of five hours every day in prayer and devotion.

Sir Henry Havelock, a distinguished British soldier, always spent the first two hours of each day alone with God. If they were to break camp at six o'clock, he would rise at four.

Earl Cairns, an Irish lawyer, rose daily at six o'clock to spend an hour and a half in Bible study and prayer, before conducting family worship at a quarter to eight.

Dr. Judson's success in God's work, as an American missionary in India, is attributable to the fact that he gave much time to prayer. He says on this point: "Arrange thy affairs, if possible, so that thou canst leisurely devote two or three hours every day, not merely to devotional exercises, but to the very act of secret prayer and communion with God. Endeavor seven times a day to withdraw from business and company, and lift up thy soul to God in private retirement. Begin the day by rising after midnight and devoting some time amid the silence and darkness of the night to this sacred work. Let the hour of opening dawn find thee at the same work. Let the hours of nine, twelve, three, six, and nine at night witness the same. Be resolute in His cause. Make all practical sacrifices to maintain it. Consider that thy time is short and that business and company must not be allowed to rob thee of thy God."

Impossible! we say. Fanatical directions! Dr. Judson impressed an empire for Christ. He laid the foundations of God's Kingdom with imperishable granite in the heart of Burma. He was successful—one of the few men who mightily impressed the world for Christ. Many men of greater gifts and genius and learning than he have made no such impression. Their religious work resembles footsteps in the sand. But, his work endures, as if it were engraved in stone. The secret of its profoundness and endurance is found in the fact that he gave time to prayer. He kept the iron red-hot with prayer, and God's skill molded it with enduring power. No man can do a great and enduring work for God who is not a man of prayer. And, no man can be a man of prayer without giving much time to prayer.

Is it true that prayer is simply a compliance with habit—dull and mechanical? Is it petty performance into which we are trained until tameness, shortness, and superficiality are its chief elements?

"Is it true that prayer is, as is assumed, little else than the half-passive play of sentiment which flows languidly on through the minutes or hours of easy reverie?" Canon Liddon, the English orator, continues: "Let those who have really prayed give the answer. They sometimes describe prayer with patriarch Jacob as a wrestling together with an Unseen Power which may last late into the night hours, or even to the break of day. Like St. Paul, they sometimes refer to common intercession as a concerted struggle. They have, when praying, their eyes fixed on the Great Intercessor in Gethsemane, on the drops of blood which fall to the ground in that agony of resignation and sacrifice. Importunity is the essence of successful prayer. Importunity means not dreaminess but sustained work. It is through prayer especially that the Kingdom of heaven suffers violence and the violent take it by force.'

It was a saying of the late Bishop Hamilton that, "A man is not likely to do much good in prayer if he does not begin by looking on it in the light of a work to be prepared for and persevered with all the earnestness which we bring to bear on subjects which in our opinion are at once more interesting and most necessary."

Chapter 7

"Early Will I Seek Thee"

I ought to pray before seeing anyone. Often when I sleep long, or meet with others early, it is eleven or twelve o'clock before I begin secret prayer. This is a wretched system. It is unscriptural. Christ arose before day and went into a solitary place. David says: "Early will I seek Thee"; "Thou shalt early hear my voice." Family prayer loses much of its power and sweetness, and I can do no good to those who come to seek from me. My conscience feels guilty, my soul unfed, my lamp not trimmed. Then, when in secret prayer, the soul is often out of tune. I feel it is far better to begin with God—to see His face first— to get my soul near Him before it is near another.

Robert Murray McCheyne

The men who have done the most for God in this world have been early on their knees. He who fritters away the early morning—its opportunity and freshness—in other pursuits than seeking God will make poor headway seeking Him the rest of the day. If God is not first in our thoughts and efforts in the morning, He will be last during the remainder of the day.

Behind this early rising and early praying is the intense desire which urges us into this pursuit after God. Morning listlessness indicates a listless heart. The heart which is lax in seeking God in the morning has lost its relish for God. David's heart was ardent after God. He hungered and thirsted after God. He sought God early before daylight. The bed and sleep could not chain his soul in its eagerness after God. Christ longed for communion with God; and so, rising a great while before day, He would go out into the mountain to pray. The disciples—when fully awake and ashamed of their indulgence—knew where to find Him. We could list men who have mightily impressed the world for God, and we would find that they were early after God.

A desire for God which cannot break the chains of sleep is a weak thing and will do little good for God. The desire for God that stays far behind the devil and the world at the beginning of the day will never catch up.

It is not simply getting up which brings men to the front and makes them leaders in God's hosts. It is the overwhelming desire which stirs and breaks all self-indulgent chains that does so. But getting up gives vent, increase, and strength to the desire. If they had lain in bed and indulged themselves, the desire would have been quenched. The desire aroused them and inspired them to reach out for God. This heeding and acting on the call gave their faith its grasp on God, and their hearts the sweetest and fullest revelation of Him. This strength of faith and fullness of revelation made them saints by eminence. The halo of their sainthood has come down to us, and we have entered into the enjoyment of their conquests. But we take our fill in enjoyment, and not in productions. We build their tombs and write their epitaphs, but are careful not to follow their examples.

We need a generation of preachers who seek God and seek Him early. We need men who give the freshness and dew of effort to God, and in return secure the freshness and fullness of His power that He may be as the dew to them—full of gladness and strength through all the heat and labor of the day. Our laziness after God is our crying sin. The children of this world are far wiser than we. They are at it early and late. We do not seek God with ardor and diligence. No man receives God who does not follow hard after Him. And, no soul follows hard after God who is not after Him in early morn.

Chapter 8

The Secret of Power

There is a manifest want of spiritual influence on the ministry of the present day. I feel it in my own case and I see it in that of others. I am afraid there is too much of a low, managing, contriving, maneuvering temper of mind among us. We are laying ourselves out more than is expedient to meet one man's taste and another man's prejudices. The ministry is a grand and holy affair, and it should find in us a simple habit of spirit and a holy but humble indifference to all consequences. The leading defect in Christian ministers is want of a devotional habit.

Richard Cecil

Never was there a greater need for saintly men and women. More imperative still is the call for saintly, God-devoted preachers. The world moves with gigantic strides. Satan has his hold and rule on the world, and labors to make all its movements subserve his ends. Christianity must do its best work, present its most attractive and perfect models. By every means, modern sainthood must be inspired by the loftiest ideals and by the largest possibilities through the Spirit.

Paul lived on his knees, so that the Ephesian church might measure the heights, breadths, and depths of an unmeasurable saintliness, and "be filled with all the fulness of God" (Ephesians 3:18-19). Epaphras laid himself out with the exhaustive toil and strenuous conflict of fervent prayer, so that the Colossian church might "stand perfect and complete in all the will of God" (Colossians 4:12). Everywhere, everything in apostolic times was growing, so that the people of God might each and "all come in the unity of faith, and of the knowledge of the Son of God, unto a perfect man, unto the measure of the stature of the fulness of Christ" (Ephesians 4:13).

No premium was given to those who fell short of God's calling. No encouragement was offered to an old babyhood. The babies were to grow. The old, instead of feebleness and infirmities, were to bear fruit in old age, and be fat and flourishing. The most divine thing in Christianity is holy men and women.

No amount of money, genius, or culture can move

things for God. Holiness energizing the soul—the whole man aflame with love, with desire for more faith, more prayer, more zeal, more consecration—this is the secret of power. These we need and must have, and men must be the incarnation of this God-inflamed devotedness. God's advance has been stayed, His cause crippled, His name dishonored for their lack. Genius (though the loftiest and most gifted), education (though the most learned and refined), position, dignity, place, and honored names cannot move this chariot of our God. It is a fiery one, and only fiery forces can move it. The genius of a Milton fails. The imperial strength of a Leo fails. But, Brainerd's spirit could move it. Brainerd's spirit was on fire for God, on fire for souls. Nothing earthly, worldly, or selfish was able to quench the intensity of this all-impelling and all-consuming force and flame.

Prayer is the creator as well as the channel of devotion. The spirit of devotion is the spirit of prayer. Prayer and devotion are united as soul and body are united, as life and heart are united. There is no real prayer without devotion, no devotion without prayer. The preacher must be surrendered to God in the holiest devotion. He is not a professional man; his ministry is not a profession. It is a divine institution, a divine devotion. He is devoted to God. His aim, aspirations, and ambitions are *for* God and *to* God; and to such, prayer is as essential as food is to life.

The preacher, above everything else, must be devoted to God. The preacher's relationship to God is the insignia and credentials of his ministry. These must be clear, conclusive, and unmistakable. His must not be a common, surface type of piety. If he does not excel in grace, he does not excel at all. If he does not preach by life, character, and conduct, he does not preach at all. His piety may be light, his preaching as soft and as sweet as music, yet, its weight will be a feather's weight—visionary, fleeting as the morning cloud or the early dew.

Devotion to God—there is no substitute for this in the preacher's character and conduct. Devotion to a church, to opinions, to an organization, to orthodoxy—these are paltry, misleading, and vain when they become the source of inspiration. God must be the mainspring of the preacher's effort, the fountain and crown of all his toil. The name and honor of Jesus Christ, the advance of His cause, must be all in all. The preacher must have no inspiration but the name of Jesus Christ, no ambition but to have Him glorified, no toil but for Him. Then, prayer will be the source of his illuminations, the means of perpetual advancement, the gauge of his success. The continual aim, the only ambition the preacher can cherish is to have God with him.

Never has God's cause been in more need of the perfect example of the possibilities of prayer than in this age. No age, no person, will demonstrate the gospel-power except the ages or persons of deep and earnest prayer. A prayerless age will have only scant models of divine power. Prayerless hearts will never rise to these glorious heights. The age may be a better age than the past. But, there is an infinite distance between the betterment of an age by the force of an advancing civilization and its betterment by the increase of holiness and Christ-likeness by the energy of prayer.

The Jews were much better off when Christ came than in the ages before. It was the golden age of their Pharisaic religion. Their golden, religious age crucified Christ. During the time before Christ, there was: never more piety, never less praying; never more indulgence, never less sacrifice; never more idolatry, never less devotion to God; never more temple worship, never less God worship; never more lip service, never less heart service; never more church-goers, never less saints.

It is the prayer force that makes saints. Holy characters are formed by the power of real praying. The more true saints, the more praying; the more praying, the more true saints.

God has now, and has had in the past, many of these devoted, prayerful preachers—men in whose lives prayer has been a mighty, controlling, conspicuous force. The world has felt their power. God has felt and honored their power. God's cause has moved mightily and swiftly by their prayers; holiness has shone out in their characters with a divine effulgence. God found one of the men he was looking for in David Brainerd, whose work and name have gone into history. He was no ordinary man, but was capable of shining in any company. He was the peer of the wise and gifted ones, eminently suited to fill the most attractive pulpits and to labor among the most refined and cultured who were so anxious to secure him for their pastor.

Jonathan Edwards, the famous missionary and clergyman, bears testimony that Brainerd was "a young man of distinguished talents, had extraordinary knowledge of men and things, had rare conversational powers, excelled in his knowledge of theory, and was truly, for one so young, an extraordinary divine, and especially in all matters relating to practical Christianity. I never knew his equal of his age and standing for clear and accurate notions of the nature and essence of true Christianity. His manner in prayer was almost inimitable, such as I have very rarely known equalled. His learning was very considerable, and he had extraordinary gifts for the pulpit."

No more noble or inspiring a story has ever been recorded in earthly annals than that of David Brainerd. No miracle attests the truth of Christianity with more divine force than the life and work of such a man. Alone in the savage wilds of America, struggling day and night with a mortal disease, unschooled in the care of souls, he fully established the worship of God. Hindered by having only a pagan interpreter through whom he preached to the

Indians, strengthened by the Word of God in his heart and in his hands, he siezed many for God's service. With his soul fired by the divine flame, and his mouth, heart, and mind always in prayer, he secured all the gracious results of his divine calling and devotion.

The Indians experienced a great change from the very lowest form of an ignorant and debased heathenism to pure, devout, intelligent Christianity. All vice was reformed; the external duties of Christianity were at once embraced and acted on. Family prayer was set up; the Sabbath was instituted and joyously observed. The internal graces of Christianity were exhibited with growing sweetness and strength.

The cause of these results is found in David Brainerd himself—not in the conditions or accidents, but in the man Brainerd. He was God's man, for God first and last and all the time. God could flow unhindered through him. The omnipotence of grace was neither arrested nor hindered by the conditions of his heart. The whole channel was broadened and cleaned out for God's fullest and most powerful passage. Thus, God, with all His mighty forces, could come down on the hopeless, savage wilderness and transform it into His blooming and fruitful garden. Nothing is too hard for God to do if He can get the right kind of man to do it.

Brainerd lived a life of holiness and prayer. His diary is full of the record of his seasons of fasting, meditation, and retirement. The time he spent in private prayer amounted to many hours daily. "When I return home," he said, "and give myself to meditation, prayer, and fasting, my soul longs for mortification, self-denial, humility and divorcement from all things of the world. I have nothing to do," he said, "with earth, but only labor in it honestly for God. I do not desire to live one minute for anything which earth can afford."

It was prayer which gave marvelous power to his life and ministry.

After this high order did he pray: "Feeling somewhat of the sweetness of communion with God and the constraining force of His love and how admirably it captivates the soul and makes all the desires and affections to center in God, I set apart this day for secret fasting and prayer to God, to direct and bless me with regard to the great work which I have in view of preaching the gospel and to ask that the Lord would return to me and show me the light of His countenance. I had little life and power in the forenoon. Near the middle of the afternoon, God enabled me to wrestle ardently in intercession for my absent friends, but just at night the Lord visited me marvelously in prayer. I think my soul was never in such agony before. I felt no restraint, for the treasures of divine grace were opened to me. I wrestled for absent friends, for the ingathering of souls, for multitudes of poor souls, and for many that I thought were the children of God, personally in many distant places. I was in such agony from sun half an hour high till near dark that I was wet all over with sweat, but yet it seemed to me I had done nothing, oh, my dear Savior did sweat blood for poor souls! I longed for more compassion toward them. I felt still in a sweet frame, under a sense of divine love and grace, and went to bed in such a frame, with my heart set on God."

The men of mighty prayer are men of spiritual strength. Prayers never die. Brainerd's whole life was a life of prayer. By day and by night he prayed. Before preaching and after preaching he prayed. Riding through the interminable solitudes of the forest he prayed. On his bed of straw he prayed. Retiring to the dense and lonely forest he prayed. Hour by hour, day after day, early morn and late at night, he was praying and fasting, pouring out his soul, interceding, communing with God. He was with God mightily in prayer; God was with him mightily, and by it, he being dead yet speaks and works, and will continue to do so until the end comes. Among the glorious ones of that glorious day, he will be with the first.

Jonathan Edwards said of him: "His life shows the right way to success in the works of the ministry. He sought it as the soldier seeks victory in a siege or battle; or as a man that runs a race for a great prize. Animated with love to Christ and souls, how did he labor? Always fervently, not only in word and doctrine, in public and in private, but in prayers by day and night, wrestling with God in secret and travailing in birth with unutterable groans and agonies, until Christ was formed in the hearts of the people to whom he was sent. Like a true son of Jacob, he persevered in wrestling through all the darkness of the night, until the breaking of the day!"

Chapter 9

Power Through Prayers

For nothing reaches the heart but what is from the heart, or pierces the conscience but what comes from a living conscience.

William Penn

In the morning I was more engaged in preparing the head than the heart. This has been frequently my error, and I have always felt the evil of it, especially in prayer. Reform it, then, O Lord! Enlarge my heart, and I shall preach.

Robert Murray McCheyne

A sermon that has more head infused into it than heart will not come home with efficacy to the hearers.

Richard Cecil

Prayer, with its manifold and many-sided forces, helps the mouth to utter the truth in its fullness and freedom. The preacher is to be prayed for, because the preacher is made by prayer. The preacher's mouth is to be prayed for—his mouth is to be opened and filled by prayer. A holy mouth is made by praying, by much praying. A brave mouth is made by praying, by much praying. The Church and the world, God and heaven, owe much to Paul's mouth. Paul's mouth owed its power to prayer.

How manifold, illimitable, valuable, and helpful prayer is to the preacher in so many ways, at so many points, in every way! One great value is, it helps his heart.

Praying makes the preacher a heart preacher. Prayer puts the preacher's whole heart into the preacher's sermon. Prayer puts the preacher's sermon into the preacher's heart.

The heart makes the preacher. Men of great hearts are great preachers. Men of bad hearts may do a measure of good, but this is rare. The hireling and the stranger may help the sheep at some points, but it is the good shepherd with the good shepherd's heart who will bless the sheep, and fill the full measure of the shepherd's place.

We have emphasized sermon preparation until we have lost sight of the important things to be prepared—the heart. A prepared heart is much better than a prepared sermon. A prepared heart will *make* a prepared sermon.

Volumes have been written stating the detailed mechanics of sermon making. We have become possessed with the idea that this scaffolding is the building. The young preacher has been taught to exhaust all of his strength on the form, taste, and beauty of his sermon as a mechanical and intellectual product. We have thereby cultivated a vicious taste among the people and raised the clamor for talent instead of grace. We have emphasized eloquence instead of piety, rhetoric instead of revelation, reputation and brilliancy instead of holiness. By it, we have lost the true idea of preaching. We have lost preaching power, and the pungent conviction for sin. We have also lost the rich experience, elevated the Christian character, and the divine authority over consciences and lives which always results from genuine preaching.

It would not do to say that preachers study too much. Some of them do not study at all; others do not study enough. Many do not study the right way to show themselves workmen approved of God. But our great lack is not in the head culture, but in heart culture. Not lack of knowledge, but lack of holiness is our sad and telling defect—not that we know too much but that we do not meditate on God and His Word, and watch and fast and pray enough. The heart is the great hindrance to our preaching. Words pregnant with divine truth find our hearts to be inconducive. Arrested, they fall flat and powerless.

Can ambition that lusts after praise and position

preach the gospel of Him who made Himself of no reputation and took on the form of a servant? Can the proud, the vain, the egotistical preach the gospel of Him who was meek and lowly? Can the bad tempered, passionate, selfish, hard, worldly man preach the doctrine which is based on longsuffering, self-denial, tenderness, and which imperatively demands separation from enmity and crucifixion to the world? Can the hireling official, heartless, perfunctory, preach the gospel which demands that the Shepherd give His life for the sheep? Can the covetous man, who counts salary and money, preach the gospel until he has cleansed his heart and can say in the spirit of Christ and Paul in the words of Wesley: "I count it dung and dross; I trample it under my feet; I (yet not I, but the grace of God in me) esteem it just as the mire of the streets, I desire it not, I seek it not"?

God's revelation does not need the light of human genius, the polish and strength of human culture, the brilliancy of human thought, the force of human brains to adorn or enforce it. But, it does demand the simplicity, docility, humility, and faith of a child's heart.

It was this surrender and subordination of intellect and genius to the divine and spiritual forces which made Paul peerless among the apostles. It was this which gave Wesley his power.

Our great need is heart preparation. Luther held it as an axiom: "He who prayed well has studied well."

We are not saying that men are not to think and use their intellects. But, he who cultivates his heart the most will use his intellect the best. We are not saying that preachers should not be students. But, we are saying that their great study should be the Bible; and, he who has kept his heart with diligence studies the Bible best. We are not saying that the preacher should not know men. But, he who has fathomed the depths and intricacies of his own heart will be more adept in the knowledge of human nature.

We are saying that while the channel of preaching is the mind, its fountain is the heart. You may broaden and deepen the channel, but if you do not look well to the purity and depth of the fountain, you will have a dry or polluted channel. Almost any man of average intelligence has sense enough to preach the gospel, but very few have grace enough to do so. He who has struggled with his own heart and conquered it—who has taught it humility, faith, love, truth, mercy, sympathy, courage; who can pour the rich treasures of the human heart thus trained all surcharged with the power of the gospel, on the consciences of his hearers—such a person will be the truest, most successful preacher in the esteem of his Lord.

The heart is the savior of the world. Heads do not save. Genius, brains, brilliancy, strength, natural gifts do not save. The gospel flows through hearts. All the mightiest forces are heart forces. All the sweetest and loveliest graces are heart graces. Great hearts make great characters; great hearts make divine characters. God is love. There is nothing greater than love, nothing greater than God. Hearts make heaven; heaven is love. There is nothing higher, nothing sweeter, than heaven. It is the heart and not the head which makes God's great preachers. The heart counts for much in every way in Christianity. The heart must speak from the pulpit. The heart must hear in the pew. In fact, we serve God with our hearts. Head homage does not conduct current in heaven.

We believe that one of the serious and most popular errors of the modern pulpit is the inclusion of more thought than prayer—more head than heart—in its sermons. Big hearts make big preachers; good hearts make good preachers. A theological school to enlarge and cultivate the heart is the golden desire of the gospel. The pastor binds his people to him and rules his people by his heart. They may admire his gifts; they may be proud of his ability; they may be affected for the time by his sermons. But, the stronghold of his power is his heart. His scepter is love. The throne of his power is his heart.

The good Shepherd gives His life for the sheep. Heads never make martyrs. It is the heart which surrenders the life to love and fidelity. It takes great courage to be a faithful pastor, but the heart alone can supply this courage. Gifts and genius may be brave, but they are the gifts and genius of the heart and not of the head.

70

It is easier to fill the head than it is to prepare the heart. It is easier to make a brain sermon than a heart sermon. It was heart that drew the Son of God from heaven. It is heart that will draw men *to* heaven. The world needs men of heart to sympathize with its woe, to kiss away its sorrows, to feel compassion for its misery, and to alleviate its pain. Christ was eminently the man of sorrows, because He was preeminently the man of heart.

"Give Me thy heart" is God's requisition of men. "Give me thy heart!" is man's demand of man.

A professional ministry is a heartless ministry. When salary plays a great part in the ministry, the heart plays little part. We may make preaching our business and not put our hearts in the business. He who puts self to the front in his preaching puts heart to the rear. He who does not sow with his heart in his study will never reap a harvest for God. The closet is the heart's study. We will learn more about how to preach and what to preach there than we can learn in our libraries. "Jesus wept" is the shortest and biggest verse in the Bible. It is he who goes forth *weeping* (not preaching great sermons), bearing precious seed, who will come again rejoicing, bringing his sheaves with him (Psalm 126:6).

Praying gives sense, brings wisdom, and broadens and strengthens the mind. The prayer closet is a perfect schoolteacher and schoolhouse for the preacher. Thought is not only brightened and clarified in prayer, but thought is born in prayer. We can

71

learn more in an hour praying, when praying indeed, than from many hours of rigorous study. There are books in the closet which can be found and read nowhere else. Revelations are made in the closet which are made nowhere else.

Chapter 10

Under the Dew of Heaven

One bright blessing which private prayer brings down upon the ministry is an indescribable and inimitable something—an anointing from the Holy One.... If the anointing which we bear comes not from the Lord of hosts, we are deceivers, since only in prayer can we obtain it. Let us continue instant, constant, fervent in supplication. Let your fleece lie on the threshing-floor of supplication till it is wet with the dew of heaven.

C.H. Spurgeon

Alexander Knox, a Christian philosopher in the days of Wesley, during the time of the great Methodist revival, writes: "It is strange and lamentable, but I verily believe the fact to be that except among Methodists and Methodistic clergymen, there is not much interesting preaching in England. The clergy, too generally, have absolutely lost the art. There is, I conceive, in the great laws of the moral world, a kind of secret understanding like the affinities in chemistry, between rightly promulgated religious truth and the deepest feelings of the human mind. Where the one is duly exhibited, the other will respond. 'Did not our hearts burn within us?'—but this devout feeling is indispensable in the speaker. Now, I am obliged to state from my own observation that this onction, as the French not unfitly term it, is beyond all comparison more likely to be found in England in a Methodist convention than in a parish church. This, and this alone, seems really to be that which fills the Methodist houses and thins the churches. I am, I verily think, no enthusiast; I am a most sincere and cordial Churchman, a humble disciple of the school of Hale and Boyle, of Burnet and Leighton. Now I must aver that when I was in this country, two years ago, I did not hear a single preacher who taught me like my own great masters but such as are deemed Methodistic. And I now despair of getting an atom of heart-instruction from any other quarter. The Methodist preachers (however I may not always approve of all their expressions) do most assuredly diffuse this religion, true and undefiled. I felt real pleasure last Sunday. I can bear witness that the preacher did at once speak the words of truth and soberness. There was no eloquence—the honest man never dreamed of such a thing but there was far better: a cordial communication of vitalized truth. I say vitalized because what he declared to others it was impossible not to feel he lived himself."

This unction or anointing is the art of preaching. The preacher who never had this anointing never had the art of preaching. The preacher who has lost this anointing has lost the art of preaching. Whatever other arts he may have and retain—the art of sermon making, the art of eloquence, the art of great, clear thinking, the art of pleasing an audience—he has lost the divine art of preaching. This anointing makes God's truth powerful and interesting, draws, attracts, edifies, convicts, and saves.

This same anointing vitalizes God's revealed truth, makes it living and life giving. Even God's truth spoken without this anointing is light, dead, and deadening. Though abounding in truth, though weighty with thought, though sparkling with rhetoric, though pointed by logic, though powerful by earnestness, without this divine anointing it issues death, not life. Mr. Spurgeon says: "I wonder how long we might beat our brains before we could plainly put into word what is meant by preaching with unction. Yet, he who preaches knows its presence, and he who hears soon detects its absence. Samaria, in famine, typifies a discourse without it. Jerusalem, with her feast of fat things, full of marrow, may represent a sermon enriched with it. Everyone knows what the freshness of the morning is when orient pearls abound on every blade of grass, but who can describe it, much less produce it of itself? Such is the mystery of spiritual anointing. We know, but we cannot tell others, what it is. It is as easy as it is foolish to counterfeit it. Unction is a thing which you cannot manufacture, and its counterfeits are worse than worthless. Yet it is, in itself, priceless, and beyond measure needful if you would edify believers and bring sinners to Christ."

Anointing is that indefinable, indescribable something which an old, renowned Scottish preacher explains thus: "There is sometimes something in preaching which cannot be described either in matter or expression, and cannot be described what it is, or from whence it cometh, but with a sweet violence it pierceth into the heart and affections and comes immediately from the Lord; but if there be any way to obtain such a thing it is by the heavenly disposition of the speaker."

We call it unction or anointing. It is this anointing which makes the Word of God "quick, and powerful, and sharper than any two-edged sword, piercing even to the dividing asunder of soul and spirit, and of the joints and marrow, and. . .a discerner of the thoughts and intents of the heart" (Hebrews 4:12). It is this anointing which gives the words of the preacher such point, sharpness, and power, and which creates such friction and stir in many a dead congregation.

The same truths have been told in the strictness of the letter, smooth as human oil could make them. But, no signs of life—not a pulse—are evident. All is as peaceful as the grave and equally as dead. The same preacher, in the meanwhile, receives a baptism of this anointing; divine inspiration is on him. The letter of the Word has been embellished and fired by this mysterious power, and the throbbings of life begin—life which receives or life which resists. The anointing pervades and convicts the conscience and breaks the heart.

This divine anointing is the feature which separates and distinguishes true gospel preaching from all other methods of presenting the truth. It creates a wide spiritual chasm between the preacher who has it and the one who does not. It supports and impregnates revealed truth with all the energy of God. Anointing is simply allowing God to be in His own Word and on His own preacher. By mighty, great, and continual prayerfulness, it is the preacher's entire potential. It inspires and clarifies his intellect, gives insight, grasp, and projecting power. It gives the preacher heart power, which is greater than head power. And, tenderness, purity, and force flow from the heart by it. Growth, freedom, fullness of thought, directness, and simplicity of utterance are the fruits of this anointing.

Often, earnestness is mistaken for this anointing. He who has the divine anointing will be earnest in the very spiritual nature of things. But, there may be a great deal of earnestness without the least bit of anointing.

Earnestness and anointing look alike from some points of view. Earnestness may be readily and without detection substituted or mistaken for unction. It requires a spiritual eye and a spiritual taste to discriminate.

Earnestness may be sincere, serious, ardent, and persevering. It goes at a thing with a good will, pursues it with perseverance, and urges it with vehemence—puts force in it. But all these forces do not rise higher than the mere human. The *man* is in it—the whole man, with all that he has of will and heart, of brains and genius, of planning, working, and talking. He has set himself to some purpose which has mastered him, and he pursues to master it. There may be none of God in it. There may be little of God in it, because there is so much of the man in it. He may present pleas in support of his earnest purpose which please, touch, move, or overwhelm with the conviction of their importance. In all this earnestness, he may move along earthly ways, being propelled by human forces only. Its altar is made by earthly hands, and its fire kindled by earthly flames.

It is said of a rather famous preacher of gifts, whose interpretation of Scripture was to his fancy or purpose, that he "grows very eloquent over his own exegesis." So men grow exceedingly earnest over their own plans or movements. Earnestness may be selfishness in disguise.

What about the anointing? It is the indefinable aspect of preaching which makes it preaching. It is that which distinguishes and separates preaching from all mere human speeches and presentations. It is the divine in preaching. It makes the preaching sharp to those who need sharpness. It cleanses as the dew those who need to be refreshed. It is well described as:

> "...a two-edged sword
> Of heavenly temper keen.
> And double were the wounds it made
> Where'er it glanced between.
> 'Twas death to sin; 'twas life
> To all who mourned for sin.
> It kindled and it silenced strife,
> Made war and peace within."

This anointing comes to the preacher not in the study but in the closet. It is heaven's distillation in answer to prayer. It is the sweetest exhalation of the Holy Spirit. It impregnates, suffuses, softens, percolates, cuts, and soothes. It carries the Word like dynamite. It makes the Word a soother, an arraigner, a revealer, a searcher. It makes the hearer a culprit or a saint—makes him weep like a child and live like a giant. It opens his heart and his purse as gently, yet as strongly as the spring opens the leaves. This anointing is not the gift of genius. It is not found in the halls of learning. No eloquence can woo it. No industry can win it. No orthodox hands can bestow it. It is the gift of God—the signet sent to His own messengers. It is heaven's knighthood given to the chosen true and brave ones who have sought this anointed honor through many hours of tearful, wrestling prayer.

Earnestness is good and impressive; genius is gifted and great. Thought kindles and inspires, but it takes a divine endowment—a more powerful energy than earnestness, genius, or thought—to break the chains of sin. It takes more to win estranged and depraved hearts to God, to repair the breaches, and to restore the Church to her old ways of purity and power. Nothing but holy anointing can do this.

In the Christian system, unction is the anointing of the Holy Spirit, separating the believer for God's work and qualifying him for it. This anointing is the one divine enablement by which the preacher accomplishes the unique and saving ends of preaching. Without it, no true spiritual results are accomplished. The results and forces in preaching do not rise above the results of unsanctified speech. Without anointing, the preacher is as potent as the pulpit.

This divine anointing on the preacher generates, through the Word of God, the spiritual results which flow from the gospel. Without this anointing, these results are not secured. Many pleasant impressions

80

may be made, but these all fall far below the ends of gospel preaching. This anointing may be simulated. There are many things that look like it. There are many results that resemble its effects. But, they are foreign to its results and to its nature. The fervor or softness excited by a pathetic or emotional sermon may look like the movements of the divine anointing. But, it has no pungent, penetrating, heartbreaking force. No heart-healing balm exists in these superficial, sympathetic, emotional movements. They are not radical—neither sin-searching nor sin-curing.

This divine anointing is the one distinguishing feature which separates true gospel preaching from all other methods of presenting truth. It backs and interpenetrates the revealed truth with all the force of God. It illumines the Word, broadens and enrichens the intellect, and empowers it to grasp and understand the Word. It qualifies the preacher's heart, and brings it to that condition of tenderness, purity, force, and light necessary to secure the highest results. This anointing gives the preacher liberty and enlargement of thought and soul—a freedom, fullness, and directness of utterance that can be secured by no other process.

Without this anointing on the preacher, the gospel has no more power to propagate itself than any other system of truth. This is the seal of its divinity. Anointing on the preacher puts God in the gospel. Without the anointing, God is absent, and the gospel is left to the low and unsatisfactory forces that the ingenuity, interest, or talents of men can devise to enforce and project its doctrines.

It is in this element that the pulpit more often fails than in any other element. It lapses just at this all-important point. It may be full of knowledge, brilliancy, eloquence, and charm. Sensationalism or less offensive methods may attract large crowds. Mental power may impress and enforce truth with all its resources. But, without this anointing, each and all of these will merely be like the fretful assault of the waters on a Gibraltar. Spray and foam may cover and spangle, but the rocks are still there, unimpressed and immoveable. The human heart can no more be rid of its hardness and sin by these human forces than these rocks can be swept away by the ocean's ceaseless flow.

This anointing is the consecration force, and its presence the continuous test of that consecration. It is this divine anointing of the preacher that secures his consecration to God and his work. Other forces and motives may call him to the work, but only this is consecration. A separation to God's work by the power of the Holy Spirit is the only consecration recognized by God as legitimate.

The anointing—the divine unction, this heavenly anointing—is what the pulpit needs and must have. This divine and heavenly oil put on it by the imposition of God's hand must soften and lubricate the whole man—heart, head, and spirit. It must mightily separate him from all earthly, secular, worldly, self-ish motives and aims, separating him to everything that is pure and God-like.

It is the presence of this anointing in the preacher which creates the stir and friction in many a congregation. The same truths have been told in the strictness of the letter, but no effect has been seen, no pain or pulsation felt. All is as quiet as a graveyard. Another preacher comes, and this mysterious influence is on him. The letter of the Word has been tried by the Spirit; the throes of a mighty movement are felt. It is the unction that pervades and stirs the conscience, and breaks the heart. Unctionless preaching makes everything hard, dry, acrid, and dead.

This anointing is more than a memory or an era of the past. It is a present, realized, conscious fact. It belongs to the experience of the man as well as to his preaching. It is that which transforms him into the image of his divine Master, as well as that by which he declares the truths of Christ with power. It is so much the power in the ministry that it makes all else seem feeble and vain without it. By its presence, it atones for the absence of all other forces.

This anointing is not an inalienable gift. It is a conditional gift. Its presence is perpetuated and increased by the same process by which it was at first secured—by unceasing prayer to God, by impassioned desires after God, by seeking it with tireless zeal, by deeming all else loss and failure without it.

This anointing comes directly from God in answer to prayer. Only praying hearts are filled with this holy oil. Only praying lips are anointed with this divine unction.

Prayer, much prayer, is the price of preaching unction. Prayer, much prayer, is the sole condition of keeping this anointing. Without unceasing prayer, the anointing never comes to the preacher. Without perseverance in prayer, the anointing, like overkept manna, breeds worms.

Chapter 11

The Example of the Apostles

Give me one hundred preachers who fear nothing but sin, and desire nothing but God, and I care not a straw whether they be clergymen or laymen; such alone will shake the gates of hell and set up the Kingdom of heaven on earth. God does nothing but in answer to prayer.

John Wesley

The apostles knew the necessity and worth of prayer to their ministry. They knew that their high commission as apostles—instead of relieving them from the necessity of prayer—committed them to it by a more urgent need. They were exceedingly jealous when some other important work exhausted their time and prevented their praying as they ought. As a result, they appointed laymen to look after the delicate and engrossing duties of ministering to the poor, so that they (the apostles) might, unhindered, give themselves "continually to prayer, and to the ministry of the word" (Acts 6:4). Prayer is put first, and their relation to prayer is put most strongly— "give themselves to it." They make a business of it, surrendering themselves to praying, putting fervor, urgency, perseverance, and time into it.

How holy, apostolic men devoted themselves to this divine work of prayer! "Night and day praying exceedingly," says Paul. "We will give ourselves continually to prayer" is the consensus of apostolic devotedness.

How these New Testament preachers laid themselves out in prayer for God's people! How they put God in full force into their churches by their praying! These holy apostles did not vainly think that they had met their high and solemn duties by faithfully delivering God's Word. But, their preaching was made effective and lasting by the fervor and insistence of their praying.

Apostolic praying was as taxing, toilsome, and

imperative as apostolic preaching. They prayed mightily day and night to bring their people to the highest regions of faith and holiness. They prayed even mightier still to hold them to this high spiritual altitude. The preacher who has never learned in the school of Christ the high and divine art of intercession for his people will never learn the art of preaching. Though homiletics be poured into him by the ton, and though he may be the most gifted genius in sermon making and sermon delivery, he will never preach as the apostles if he does not pray as they did.

The prayers of apostolic, saintly leaders do much in making saints of those who are not apostles. If the church leaders in later years had been as particular and fervent in praying for their people as the apostles were, the sad, dark times of worldliness and apostasy would not have marred the history of the world, and arrested the advance of the Church. Apostolic praying makes apostolic saints, and keeps apostolic times of purity and power in the Church.

Chapter 12

What God Would Have

If some Christians who have been complaining of their ministers had said and acted less before men and had applied themselves with all their might to cry to God for their ministers—had, as it were, risen and stormed heaven with their humble, fervent, and incessant prayers for them—they would have been much more in the way of success.

Jonathan Edwards

Somehow the practice of praying for the preacher has fallen into disuse, or become discounted. Occasionally, we have heard the practice referred to as a discredit of the ministry. Some think of it as being a public declaration of the inefficiency of the ministry. Perhaps praying for the preacher offends the pride of learning and self-sufficiency. But, these *ought* to be offended and rebuked if a ministry is so derelict as to allow them to exist.

Prayer, to the preacher, is not simply the duty of his profession—a privilege. It is a necessity. Air is not more necessary to the lungs than prayer is to the preacher. It is absolutely necessary for the preacher to pray. It is an absolute necessity that the preacher be prayed for. These two propositions are wedded into a union which ought never to know any divorce. *The preacher must pray; the preacher must be prayed for.* It will take all the praying he can do, and all the praying he can get done, to meet the fearful responsibilities and gain the largest, truest success in his great work. The true preacher, next to the cultivation of the spirit and fact of prayer in himself in their most intense form, greatly covets the prayers of God's people.

The more holy a man is, the more he estimates prayer; the clearer he sees that God gives Himself to the praying ones, and that the measure of God's revelation to the soul is proportionate to the soul's longing, importunate prayer for God. Salvation never finds its way to a prayerless heart. The Holy

Spirit never abides in a prayerless spirit. Preaching never edifies a prayerless soul. Christ knows nothing of prayerless Christians. The gospel cannot be extended by a prayerless preacher. Gifts, talents, education, eloquence, and God's call cannot lessen the demand of prayer, but only intensify the necessity for the preacher to pray and to be prayed for. The more the preacher's eyes are opened to the nature, responsibility, and difficulties in his work, the more he will see. And, if he is a true preacher, he will feel the necessity of prayer even more strongly. He will not only feel the increasing demand to pray himself, but to call on others to help him by their prayers.

What loftiness of soul, what purity and elevation of motive, what unselfishness, what self-sacrifice, what exhaustive toil, what enthusiasm of spirit, what divine tact are necessary to be an intercessor for men!

The preacher is to lay himself out in prayer for his people—not that they might simply be saved, but that they be mightily saved. The apostles laid themselves out in prayer so that their sights might be perfect. They did this not because they wanted a meager relish for the things of God, but so that they "might be filled with all the fullness of God" (Ephesians 3:19). Paul did not rely on his apostolic preaching to secure this end. For this cause, he bowed his knees to the Father of our Lord Jesus Christ (Ephesians 3:14). Paul's praying carried Paul's converts farther along the highway of sainthood than Paul's preaching did. Epaphras did as much or more by prayer for the Colossian saints than by his preaching. He labored fervently always in prayer for them that they might "stand perfect and complete in all the will of God" (Colossians 4:12).

Preachers are preeminently God's leaders. They are primarily responsible for the condition of the Church. They shape its character, give tone and direction to its life.

Much depends on these leaders. They shape the times and the institutions. The Church is divine; the treasure it incases is heavenly. But, it bears the imprint of the human. The treasure is in earthen vessels, and it tastes of the vessel. The Church of God makes, or is made by, its leaders. In any case, the Church will be what its leaders are: spiritual if they are so; secular if they are; conglomerate if its leaders are.

Israel's kings gave character to Israel's piety. A church rarely revolts against or rises above the religion of its leaders. Strong spiritual leaders—men of holy might—at the lead are tokens of God's favor. Disaster and weakness follow the wake of feeble or worldly leaders. Israel fell low when God gave them children for princes and babes to rule over them. The prophets predict unhappiness when children oppress God's Israel and enemies rule over them. Times of spiritual leadership are times of great spiritual prosperity to the Church.

Prayer is one of the eminent characteristics of strong spiritual leadership. Men of mighty prayer are men of might, and they shape the outcome of things. Their power with God has the conquering tread.

How can a man who does not get his message fresh from God in the closet expect to preach? How can he preach without having his faith quickened, his vision cleared, and his heart warmed by his closeting with God? Alas for the pulpit lips which are untouched by this closet flame! They will forever be dry and without the anointing. Divine truths will never come with power from such lips. As far as the real interests of Christianity are concerned, a pulpit without a closet will always be a barren thing.

A preacher may preach in an official, entertaining, or learned way, without prayer. But, there is an immeasurable distance between this kind of preaching and the sowing of God's precious seed with holy hands and prayerful, weeping hearts.

Paul is an illustration of these things. If any man could extend or advance the gospel by personal force, by brain power, by culture, by personal grace, by God's apostolic commission, God's extraordinary call, that man was Paul. Paul exemplifies the fact that the preacher must be a man given to prayer. Paul preeminently demonstrates that the true apostolic preacher must have the prayers of other good people to give to his ministry its full quota of success. He asks, he covets, he pleads in an impassioned way for the help of all God's saints. He knew that in the spiritual realm—as elsewhere—in union there is strength. He knew that the concentration and aggregation of faith, desire, and prayer increased the volume of spiritual force until it became overwhelming and irresistible in its power. Units of prayer combined, like drops of water, make an ocean which defies resistance. So Paul, with his clear and full understanding of spiritual dynamics, decided to make his ministry as impressive, eternal, and irresistible as the ocean by gathering all the scattered units of prayer and precipitating them on his ministry.

The reason for Paul's prominence in labors and results, and his impact on the Church and the world, may be that he was able to center more prayer on himself and his ministry than others. To his brethren at Rome he wrote: "Now I beseech you, brethren, for the Lord Jesus Christ's sake, and for the love of the Spirit, that ye strive together with me in your prayers to God for me" (Romans 15:30).

To the Ephesians he says: "Praying always with all prayer and supplication in the Spirit, and watching thereunto with all perseverance and supplication for all saints; and for me, that utterance may be given unto me, that I may open my mouth boldly, to make known the mystery of the gospel" (Ephesians 6:18-19).

To the Colossians he emphasizes: "Withal praying also for us, that God would open unto us a door of utterance, to speak the mystery of Christ, for which I am also in bonds: that I may make it manifest, as I ought to speak" (Colossians 4:3-4).

To the Thessalonians he says sharply, strongly: "Brethren, pray for us" (1 Thessalonians 5:25).

Paul calls on the Corinthian church to help him: "Ye also helping together by prayer for us" (2 Corinthians 1:11). This was to be part of their work. They were to lay to the helping hand of prayer.

Paul, in an additional and closing charge to the Thessalonian church about the importance and necessity of their prayers, says: "Finally, brethren, pray for us, that the word of the Lord may have free course, and be glorified, even as it is with you: and that we may be delivered from unreasonable and wicked men" (2 Thessalonians 3:1-2).

He impresses upon the Philippians that all his trials and opposition can be made subservient to the spread of the gospel by the efficiency of their prayers for him. Philemon was to prepare a lodging for him, for, through Philemon's prayer, Paul was to be his guest.

Paul's attitude about this question illustrates his humility and his deep insight into the spiritual forces which project the gospel. More than this, it teaches a lesson for all times—that if Paul was so dependent on the prayers of God's saints to give his ministry success, how much greater the necessity that the prayers of God's saints be centered on the ministry of today!

Paul did not feel that this urgent plea for prayer lowered his dignity, lessened his influence, or depreciated his piety. What if it did? Let dignity go; let influence be destroyed; let his reputation be marred—he must have their prayers. Called, commissioned, chief of the apostles as he was, all his equipment was imperfect without the prayers of his people. He wrote letters everywhere, urging them to pray for him. Do you pray for your preacher? Do you pray for him in secret? Public prayers are of little worth unless they are founded on or followed up by private praying. The praying ones are to the preacher as Aaron and Hur were to Moses. They hold up his hands and decide the issue that is so fiercely raging around them.

The plea and purpose of the apostles were to stir the Church to praying. They did not ignore the grace of cheerful giving. They were not ignorant of the place which religious activity and work occupied in the spiritual life. But, not one or all of these, in apostolic estimate or urgency, could at all compare in necessity and importance with prayer. The most sacred and urgent pleas were used—the most fervid exhortation—the most comprehensive and arousing words were uttered to enforce the all-important obligation and necessity of prayer.

"Put the saints everywhere to praying" is the burden of the apostolic effort and the keynote of apostolic success. Jesus Christ strove to do this in the days of His personal ministry. As He was moved by infinite compassion at the ripened fields of the earth perishing for lack of laborers—and pausing in His own praying—He tries to awaken the sensibilities of His disciples to the duty of prayer as He charges them, "Pray ye therefore the Lord of the harvest, that He will send forth laborers into His harvest" (Matthew 9:38). "And He spake a parable unto them to this end, that men ought always to pray, and not to faint" (Luke 18:1).

Our devotions are not measured by the clock, but time is of their essence. The ability to wait and stay and press essentially belongs to our fellowship with God. Haste, everywhere unseeming and damaging, is often, to an alarming extent, a part of the great business of communion with God. Short devotions are the bane of deep piety. Calmness, grasp, and strength are never the companions of haste. Short devotions deplete spiritual vigor, arrest spiritual progress, sap spiritual foundations, and blight the root and bloom of the spiritual life. They are the prolific source of backsliding, the sure indication of a superficial piety; they deceive, blight, rot the seed, and impoverish the soil.

It is true that Bible prayers in word and print are short, but the praying men of the Bible were with God through many sweet and holy, wrestling hours. They won by few words but long waiting. The prayers Moses records may be short, but Moses prayed to God with fastings and mighty cryings forty days and nights.

The statement of Elijah's praying may be condensed to a few brief paragraphs. But doubtless, Elijah, who when "praying he prayed," spent many hours of fiery struggle and lofty communion with God before he could, with assured boldness, say to Ahab, "There shall not be dew nor rain these years, but according to my word" (1 Kings 17:1). The Bible record of Paul's prayers is short, but Paul prayed night and day exceedingly (1 Thessalonians 3:10).

The Lord's Prayer is a divine epitome for infant lips, but Christ Jesus often prayed all night before His work was done. And, His all night and long-sustained devotions gave His work its finish and perfection, and His character the fullness and glory of its divinity.

Spiritual work is taxing work, and men are loath to do it. Praying—true praying—costs an outlay of serious attention and time, which flesh and blood do not relish. Few people are made of such strong fiber that they will make a costly outlay when inferior work will pass just as well in the market. We can habituate ourselves to our beggarly praying until it looks well to us. At least it presents a decent front and quiets the conscience—the deadliest of opiates! We can become lax in our praying, and not realize the peril until the damage has been done. Hasty devotions make weak faith, feeble convictions, and questionable piety. To be little *with* God is to be little *for* God. To cut the praying short makes the whole Christian character short, miserly, and slovenly.

It takes much time for the fullness of God to flow into the spirit. Short devotions cut the pipe of God's full flow. It takes time spent in the secret places to receive the full revelation of God. Little time and hurry mar the picture.

Henry Martyn, the English missionary, laments that "want of private devotional reading and shortness of prayer through incessant sermon-making had produced much strangeness between God and my soul." He judged that he had dedicated too much time to *public* ministrations and too little to *private* communion with God. He was very impressed with the need to set apart and devote time for fasting and solemn prayer. Resulting from this, he records: "Was assisted this morning to pray for two hours." Said William Wilberforce, the peer of kings: "I must secure more time for private devotions. I have been living far too public for me. The shortening of private devotions starves the soul; it grows lean and faint. I have been keeping too late hours." Of a failure in Parliament he says: "Let me record my grief and shame, and all, probably, from private devotions having been contracted, and so God let me stumble." More solitude and earlier hours were his remedy.

More time and early hours devoted to prayer would revive and invigorate many a decayed spiritual life. More time and early hours for prayer would be manifest in holy living. A holy life would not be so rare or so difficult a thing if our devotions were not so short and hurried. A Christly temper, in its sweet and passionless fragrance, would not be so alien and hopeless a heritage if our closet stay were lengthened and intensified. We live shabbily because we pray meagerly. Plenty of time to feast in our closets will bring marrow and fatness to our lives. Our ability to stay with God in our closet directly relates to our ability to stay with God out of the closet. Hasty closet visits are deceptive and defaulting. We are not only deluded by them, but we are losers by them in many ways and in many rich legacies. Tarrying in the closet instructs and wins. We are taught by it, and the greatest victories are often the results of great waiting—waiting until words and plans are exhausted. Silent and patient waiting gains the crown. Jesus Christ asks with an affronted emphasis, "Shall not God avenge His own elect, which cry day and night unto Him?" (Luke 18:7).

To pray is the greatest thing we can do; and to do it well there must be calmness, time, and deliberation. Otherwise, it is degraded into the smallest and meanest of things. True praying has the largest results for good; and poor praying, the least. We cannot do too much real praying; we cannot do too little of the imitation. We must learn anew the worth of prayer—enter anew the school of prayer. There is nothing which it takes more time to learn. And, if we want to learn the wondrous art, we must not offer a fragment here and there—"A little talk with Jesus," as the tiny saintlets sing. But, we must demand and hold with an iron grasp the best hours of the day for God and prayer, or there will be no praying worth the name.

This, however, is not a day of prayer. Few men pray. Prayer is defamed by preacher and priest. In these days of hurry and bustle, of electricity and steam, men will not take time to pray. There are preachers who "say prayers" as a part of their program, on regular or state occasions. But, who "stirreth up himself to take hold upon God" (Isaiah 64:7)? Who prays as Jacob prayed—till he is crowned as a prevailing, princely intercessor? Who prays as Elijah prayed—till all the locked-up forces of nature were unsealed and a famine-stricken land bloomed as the garden of God? Who prays as Jesus Christ prayed, as out upon the mountain He "continued all night in prayer to God" (Luke 6:12)? The apostles "gave themselves continually to prayer" (Acts 6:4)—the most difficult thing to get men or even the preachers to do.

There are laymen who will give their money—some of them in rich abundance—but they will not give themselves to prayer, without which their money is only a curse. There are plenty of preachers who will preach and deliver great and eloquent addresses on the need of revival and the spread of the Kingdom of God. But, there are many who will do that without prayer which makes all preaching and organizing worse than vain. Prayer is out of date—almost a lost art. The greatest benefactor this age could have is the man who will bring the preachers and the Church back to prayer.

The apostles could only glimpse the great importance of prayer before Pentecost. But the Spirit coming and filling at Pentecost elevated prayer to its vital and all-commanding position in the gospel of Christ. Now, the call of prayer to every saint is the Spirit's loudest and most urgent call. Sainthood's piety is made, refined, and perfected by prayer. The gospel moves with slow and timid pace when the saints are not at their prayers early and late and long.

Where are the Christ-like leaders who can teach the modern saints how to pray and put them at it? Do we know that we are raising up a prayerless set of saints? Where are the apostolic leaders who can put God's people to praying? Let them come to the front and do the work, and it will be the greatest work which can be done. An increase in educational facilities and a great increase in money will be the direct curse to Christianity if they are not sanctified by more and better praying than we are doing.

More praying will not come as a matter of course. The campaign for the twentieth or thirtieth century fund will hinder our praying if we are not careful. Nothing but a specific effort from a praying leadership will avail. The chief ones must lead in the apostolic effort to radicate the vital importance and *fact* of prayer in the heart and life of the Church. Only praying leaders can have praying followers. Praying apostles will beget praying saints. A praying pulpit will beget praying pews. We greatly need somebody who can set the saints to this business of praying. We are not a generation of praying saints. Non-praying saints are a beggarly gang of saints who have neither the zeal nor the beauty nor the power of saints. Who will restore this breach? He who can set the Church to praying will be the greatest of reformers and apostles.

We put it as our most sober judgement that the great need of the Church in this and all ages is men of commanding faith, unsullied holiness, marked spiritual vigor, and consuming zeal. Their prayers, faith, lives, and ministry will be of such a radical and aggressive form as to work spiritual revolutions which will form eras in individual and church life.

We do not need men who arouse sensational stirs by novel devices, nor those who attract by a pleasing entertainment. But, we need men who can stir things, work revolutions by the preaching of God's Word, and, by the power of the Holy Spirit, cause revolutions which change the whole current of events. Natural ability and educational advantages do not figure as factors in this matter. But, capacity for faith, the ability to pray, the power of thorough consecration, and the ability of self-littleness are all important factors. Also required are an absolute losing of one's self in God's glory and an ever present and insatiable yearning and seeking after all the fullness of God. We need men who can set the Church ablaze for God—not in a noisy, showy way, but with an intense and quiet heat which melts and moves everything for God.

God can work wonders if He has a suitable man. Men can work wonders if they let God lead them. The full endowment of the Spirit which turned the world upside down would be eminently useful in these latter days. Men who can stir things mightily for God, whose spiritual revolutions change the whole aspect of things, are the universal need of the Church.

The Church has never been without these men. They adorn its history. They are the standing miracles of the divinity of the Church. Their example and history are an unfailing inspiration and blessing. An increase in their number and power should be our prayer.

That which has been done in spiritual matters can be done again, and be better done. This was Christ's view. He said: "Verily, verily, I say unto you, He that believeth on me, the works that I do shall he do also; and greater works than these shall he do; because I go unto my Father" (John 14:12).

The past has not exhausted the possibilities nor the demands for doing great things for God. The church that is dependent on its past history for its miracles of power and grace is a fallen church.

God wants elect men—men of whom self and the world have been severely crucified. Their bankruptcy has so totally ruined self and the world that there is neither hope nor desire of recovery. God wants men who by this insolvency and crucifixion have turned toward Him with perfect hearts.

Let us pray ardently that God's promise to prayer may be more than realized.